Churchill's England

Churchill's England

BY ADELE GUTMAN NATHAN

FIEL PERO DESDICHADO

PUBLISHERS Grosset & Dunlap NEW YORK

MANUFACTURED IN THE UNITED STATES OF AMERICA

LIBRARY OF CONGRESS CATALOG CARD NUMBER: 63-18971

Foreword

His full name is Winston Leonard Spencer Churchill. But for years and years, even after he became Prime Minister of England, everybody spoke of him as "Winston."

Almost all his life Winston was famous.

When he was just twenty-one, people on both sides of the Atlantic Ocean were reading Winston's newspaper stories about his adventures in Cuba. The first of the many books he has written became a best seller before he was twenty-five. He was a handsome war hero and his photograph — in a campaign hat turned up on the side — was on the bureaus of teenagers before he was thirty. Cartoons of his political goings on appeared in *Punch*, the great English weekly magazine and were widely copied, before he was forty. The speeches he was making at the same time in the British House of Commons were used as models by college students in their debating societies. He was bitterly attacked — and defended — during World War I. His lectures were enthusiastically attended and his new books read in the years that followed.

And when in World War II, England fought alone, Winston was his countrymen's dauntless leader and became the inspiration for the whole Free World.

Many changes took place in Winston's England during his long life. Two years after he was born, Alexandrina Victoria, Queen of the United Kingdom and Ireland, was proclaimed Empress of India. This was the period of England's greatest power, when "the sun never set" on her domain. During these years, the English went out as colonizers to the farthest ends of the earth. They brought with them English justice, English education, English religion, and English customs. They pushed railroads through jungles, brought new industries into the wastelands, unearthed the untapped mineral wealth of the still underdeveloped regions of Asia, Africa, the Middle East, and the islands of the Pacific. English benevolence and English rule went hand in hand, and England herself became immensely powerful and immensely prosperous.

Victoria's son, Edward VII, carried on the work of spreading English influence and acquiring new territories. The British Empire and the British Commonwealth of Nations grew and grew until it became the most successful commercial combine ever known — a worldwide "Common Market" of the day.

Edward's son, George V, defended the Empire against the threat of the new Germany in World War I, and his sons, Edward VIII in his short reign and George VI in World War II, carried on the great Victorian tradition. After Victoria's great great-granddaughter, Elizabeth II, came to the throne, the former English colonies, one by one, began to be given their independence. Then, by their own choosing, many of them elected to become members of the British Commonwealth of Nations.

Through all these changes, Winston Churchill played an important part. And as year succeeded year, he became more famous, more distinguished, and more beloved by people all over the world.

The Battle of Blenheim, 1704, in which the first Duke of Marlborough and Prince Eugene defeated the French.

Contents

ACKNOWLEDGMENT

For their courtesy and cooperation in supplying the pictures on the pages indicated, the author gives grateful acknowledgment to the following:

WIDE WORLD PHOTOS: Pages 19, 29, 39, 40, 44, 45, 46-47, 56, 57, 59, 60, 61, 63, 65, 70, 74 (2 pictures), 75, 76, 77 (2 pictures), 78-79, 81, 83 (2 pictures), 84-85, 86 (2 pictures), 87, 88, 89, 90, 91 (2 pictures), 93.

NEW YORK PUBLIC LIBRARY PICTURE COLLECTION: Pages 9, 16, 17, 18, 24, 27, 29, 30, 34, 38, 42, 54, 58, 66, 72, 73, 92.

THE BETTMANN ARCHIVE: Pages 10, 16, 17, 21, 22-23, 36-37, 43, 47, 51, 67, 68, 71.

PIX, INC.: Back Endsheet photograph.

CHARLES PHELPS CUSHING: Pages 48, 80. Photographs by Alice Chauncey.

CULVER PICTURES, INC.: Front Endsheet, Pages 14, 15, 16, 20, 25, 26, 33, 35, 41, 45, 53, 56 (2 pictures), 62, 64, 82, 82-83.

Churchill's England

I. Born in a Palace

On the night of November 30, 1874, at Blenheim Palace, in England, the seventh Duke of Marlborough was holding a great ball. Among his guests were his son, Lord Randolph Churchill, and his son's young wife.

Suddenly, while the gaiety was at its height, Lady Randolph was rushed from the ballroom into a little cloakroom where some of the ladies had left their wraps.

There, surrounded by velvet cloaks and feather boas, Winston Churchill was born.

The great palace where Winston came into the world had been built in 1705 for his ancestor, John Churchill, during the reign of Queen Anne. It was a gift of the grateful people of England.

John Churchill had been an important figure in English politics. But more than this, he had been a brilliant and successful British general. The palace had its name from one of his most famous victories — the Battle of Blenheim. Because of his military record, Queen Anne made John Churchill the first Duke of Marlborough.

Winston's mother wasn't English. She was a beautiful, gay American, born Jennie Jerome in Brooklyn, New York. While she was still in her teens, Jennie and her older sister were the belles of New York City's fashionable society. Both of them had many, many American beaux.

Mrs. Jerome often took her daughters traveling in Europe. They were just as popular in Paris as they were in America. And when they went to London to escape the Franco-Prussian War, they were a social success in the British capital, too.

The top event in the London social whirl was the regatta at Cowes. The Prince of Wales went there in his yacht, as did all the dukes and earls of England who could afford such expensive pleasures. Many of the crowned heads of Europe came, too.

During the day the brilliant society watched sailing races, and in the evening they attended the most lavish parties.

A regatta at Cowes.

[15]

...rtrait of John Churchill, the first Duke, as a knight ...armor. Probably painted by Sir Godfrey Kneller.

Lord and Lady Randolph Churchill were always *dressed in the height of fashion.*

BETTMANN ARCH

One summer, Mrs. Jerome and her two beautiful daughters were invited to join a yachting party at Cowes. Among all the ladies there was none who outshone the two American girls.

The first day of the festivities, Jennie Jerome met Lord Randolph Churchill, third son of the seventh Duke of Marlborough.

It was love at first sight. They were married after a whirlwind courtship.

Randolph Churchill did everything in a whirlwind. He had a way of speaking his mind no matter what happened. Even as a schoolboy at Eton, and as a student at Oxford University, he got into

[16]

In 1963, the palatial home of the Leonard Jeromes was still standing on the corner of 26th Street facing Madison Square in New York City.

"scrapes." But he was so good-natured that most people forgave him.

He was always in the news. He drove his own trotting horses and raced them in the public parks and city streets against other "young bloods" who were his friends. His thoroughbred horses and his jockeys, wearing the Churchill colors, often won the races at Ascot and Epsom.

Lord and Lady Randolph led a very gay life. They went to house parties in Scotland, and to balls and dinners and hunt meets, or they were off on yachting trips in the Mediterranean Sea. They didn't have much time to spend in the nursery, but all his life Winston adored his beautiful mother and admired his brilliant father, even though he didn't see much of them while he was growing up. His father became his hero.

His other lifelong hero was the first Duke of Marlborough.

Winston often went visiting at Blenheim Palace where he had been born. There he heard stories of how his ancestor, through his exploits, had made England the most important of all the European powers. Winston grew up wishing that he, too, might someday do something for his country, and add to Britain's glory.

The toys he liked best were lead soldiers in English uniforms. As his lead army grew bigger and bigger, Mrs. Everest, his nurse, set up a big

Winston's years of service spanned more than four generations of royalty. Left to right: Edward VII, Edward VIII (now the Duke of Windsor), Queen Victoria, George V. BETTMANN ARCHIVE

table in his nursery. Here on this battlefield, Winston marshaled his soldiers in military formation. He pretended he was a famous general leading his men into battle. From the time he was very young, he was determined to make his mark in the world like his father and his ancestor.

The little room in Blenheim where Winston Churchill was born. (Restored).
Winston's baby vest is on display for tourists to see.

W.S. CHURCHILL
BABY'S
VEST
DO NOT TOUCH

Winston Churchill at 15, with his mother and his brother Jack.

II. Ireland

A short time after Winston's fourth birthday, Queen Victoria appointed his grandfather, the seventh Duke of Marlborough, Lord-Lieutenant of Ireland. The duke invited his son, Lord Randolph, to come with him to Dublin as his secretary.

It just happened that Randolph Churchill was in one of his "scrapes" again. In his usual frank style, he had spoken his mind about the behavior of a very close friend of the Prince of Wales.

The Prince of Wales heard about Lord Randolph's remarks. He was very much displeased. He decided to teach Randolph a lesson.

So he let it be known that he would refuse to accept any invitations to any social events at which he might meet the Churchills. London society was in a ticklish spot. Most people liked the Randolph Churchills. They added so much to the gaiety of a ball or a dinner. She was beautiful, well dressed, and witty, and he was handsome and entertaining.

But to have the Prince of Wales accept an invitation was the ambition of every social leader. The Churchills were dropped from many party lists, and life in London lost much of its glitter for them.

So the chance to go to Ireland was welcomed. The whole Randolph Churchill family moved to Dublin.

It was a big job — pulling up stakes. There were so many things and people to be taken along. Lady Randolph was afraid she could not find satisfactory domestic servants to suit her in another country. And Lord Randolph wanted to make sure that his precious horses had the proper kind of attention. So they took kitchen help and butlers, personal maids, valets, parlormaids, grooms, jockeys, and horses with them, and the fine linen sheets, pillows, towels, and table linen embroidered with the Churchill coat of arms.

In addition to all this, there were little Winston and Mrs. Everest, his nanny, and all the things that were needed for the nursery.

Winston had a wonderful time watching the movers. He wasn't allowed to take along his lead soldiers. But he promised them that he would be back soon and would not forget about them. In

Blarney Castle, Ireland.

the days following, he had all the pleasures of a trip on a boat across the Irish Sea.

The Viceregal Lodge in Dublin stood in a big park surrounded by a high wall. The Duke of Marlborough gave beautiful lawn parties there.

Lady Randolph, as always, was the outstanding beauty at the parties. And since in Dublin the Viceroy, not the Prince of Wales, was the leader of society, everybody who was anybody accepted

A visit to the Blarney Stone in County Cork, Ireland.

the duke's daughter-in-law's invitations and tried to outdo each other in entertaining the Churchills.

Winston's parents lived in a constant whirl of hunt breakfasts, pheasant shoots, dinners, and balls. They were asked to visit all the historic Irish castles. Lady Randolph even journeyed to the west of Ireland to kiss the Blarney Stone. Since one has to be lowered upside down to reach the Blarney Stone, this athletic feat of Lady Randolph made her very popular with the local gentry.

Winston, of course, did not go on these trips with his parents. There was plenty of room for him to ride his pony and drive around in his cart and play without having to go outside the wall that surrounded Phoenix Park. It was a wonderful place for a child to play.

When he did go out beyond the wall, it wasn't so pleasant. Every now and then Mrs. Everest would decide to take the little boy on a trip to town. Winston never forgot how the people in the streets crowded around them and called out in ugly voices. He was puzzled. Why were they so angry? What had he done wrong?

When Winston was older, he learned more about the reason for their anger.

He learned that back in the twelfth century, the overlordship of Ireland had been granted to Henry II of England by Pope Adrian IV. But the Irish people would not accept English rule, and in 1169, an English army invaded Ireland. The struggle for control went on. During more than six centuries the English Crown had always had to maintain large armies in Ireland at great expense.

When Oliver Cromwell was a ruler in England, he waged a particularly cruel and bloody war against the Irish. He pursued with especial harshness the old practice of seizing farms in the fertile North of Ireland and giving them to settlers

Winston's mother took him to this garden party in Richmond, near London, in 1886.

he brought over from Scotland. The Scotch-Irish were hard working and earnest and did very well with the farms and prospered.

The Irish who were pushed out of their farms had nowhere to go but to the South. Here the land was rocky and barren. But even in the South they could find no places of their own. For Cromwell had divided most of the big estates among the English who had helped him in the campaign,

and the dispossessed Irish were forced to rent their poor little farms from the new English owners.

Since the English owners almost never came to Ireland, the peasants had to deal with them through agents.

These estate agents, although most of them were Irish themselves, nevertheless were hard on their fellow countrymen. They wanted to make a good showing with their English bosses. When a little

The Scotch-Irish always opposed Home Rule. Today the North of Ireland is still a part of the United Kingdom tho

farmer got behind in his rent, everything he had was taken from him and he was likely to be thrown off his farm — a pauper.

The peasants' farms were very small, and the renters did not know how to plant them so that they would pay. The biggest crop was potatoes, and when the potato crop failed, there would be dreadful poverty and even famine among the Irish.

| 22 |

North and the pauperized South. To make things more difficult, the Scotch-Irish and the Irish-Irish did not even have the same religion.

Ireland originally had its own Parliament, but in 1800 this had been abolished, and now members representing the Irish counties sat in the English Parliament in London. The Scotch-Irish sent their own delegates. Naturally, they were satisfied with the kind of government they were getting.

But the people in the South were represented, not by their own people, but by the landlords. The Irish leaders started a movement to get a Parliament of their own again in Dublin. They wanted "Dominion Status" as Canada had in North America.

These leaders called their movement "The Irish Home Rule." Home Rule was a hot subject in the English Parliament.

When Winston and his family were living in Dublin the Irish people were having very bad times indeed. Many of the peasants who had been thrown off their farms had come to the city to look for jobs, but they couldn't find jobs. They couldn't even find places to live. They squatted on the outskirts of the city in miserable shacks made of whatever they could find, and they lived by begging.

The Irish blamed all their troubles on the English. Since Winston's grandfather, the Lord Lieutenant of Ireland, was English, they hated him and all his family.

But, of course, at the time, Winston was too young to understand all this.

South has become the Republic of Eire.

The English owners, who never saw the farms, did not understand all this. So they did practically nothing to help their tenants.

Ireland was like two countries — the prosperous

III. Latin and the Three R's

When Winston was seven, the whole family and the servants and the baggage and the horses went back to England. The Prince of Wales seemed to have forgotten all about his displeasure and welcomed the amusing Randolph Churchills back into his circle. Winston was delighted to see his own nursery again and to find his soldiers still standing on the table waiting for him to lead them into battle.

There was a new excitement in the Churchill household. Lord Randolph had made up his mind to "stand" for a seat in the House of Commons. (In America, we say a man "runs" for office. In England he "stands.")

The House of Commons in the English Parliament is the Lower House, something like the House of Representatives in the American Congress. The English House of Lords is something like the American Senate.

The dukes and earls and barons of England, Ireland, and Scotland who sit in the House of Lords inherit their seats. Lord Randolph's father, the seventh Duke of Marlborough, was in the House of Lords.

The M.P.'s, Members of the Lower House, are elected by the people.

At that time, the M.P.'s didn't get any salary. They even had to spend a lot of their own money on their campaigns. So almost all the Members of Commons were from the rich "upper" classes, like Lord Randolph Churchill.

Lord Randolph went campaigning. He went to speak at meetings in the evenings, and during the day he drove around stopping to shake hands with people and asking them to vote for him. Lady Randolph went right along with him. She loved doing it and was very popular.

All this excitement hardly touched little Winston. He went on playing with his soldiers in the nursery wing of the house, and being spoiled by his nanny. He saw his parents less frequently than ever, but he was enjoying his life.

And then suddenly, all his good times came to an end. He was sent to school. In those days, there

Eton College, where Lord Randolph went to school, and Harrow, where Winston spent four and a half years, are called public schools. In the United States they would be classed as private schools because the pupils pay tuition.

At seven, Winston wore a sailor suit, but he was more interested in soldiers than in sailors.

Rugby is the football of England, but Winston never liked to play it.

was nothing unusual about sending little boys of seven away alone to boarding school.

The English boarding schools were very strict. The boys were made to obey the rules. Even the smallest boys had to study Latin and Greek. If they did not do well in their lessons, they were "birched," that is, they were whipped with a long, thin birch rod until they promised to work harder.

No teacher ever explained what all the rules were for. And Winston just couldn't obey rules that he did not understand. All the birching in the world didn't seem to make him learn to write Latin. He wasn't much good at mathematics either. He just managed to scrape through — almost always low boy in his class.

He loved English, whether prose or poetry. His favorite books were adventure stories. He read *Treasure Island* and *King Solomon's Mines* over and over again. He got hold of a book of poems called *Lays of Ancient Rome* by Thomas Macaulay.

One of the poems especially thrilled him. It was called "Horatius at the Bridge" and told about a noble Roman soldier who stood on a bridge over the Tiber River and, single-handed, kept the Etruscan foes from crossing until the last Roman soldier was safe on the other side.

Winston learned this poem by heart. And he learned all the other poems in the book, twelve hundred in all, and recited them in class. Everybody was astonished. It was certainly amazing for a boy at the foot of his class to be able to perform such a feat.

The secret was that Winston had a marvelous memory when he wanted to use it. It was this unusual memory that made him get through school at all.

Winston was not even good at the usual school games. He never could learn to play soccer, but he was a fine swimmer and a splendid horseman.

His parents, especially his father, were not very pleased with his school record. It never occurred to them that maybe he was only copying *them*, in being so self-willed and wanting to do only the things that he enjoyed.

As an M.P., Lord Randolph was famous for his own independent behavior. He had become the Leader of the House and Chancellor of the Exchequer. As Chancellor, he managed the money for the Government. He was very outspoken in his criticism of Government spending. This was very embarrassing to the Prime Minister, who naturally thought that his own Cabinet Ministers should follow his lead.

But Lord Randolph would not follow anybody's lead. The newspapers took to calling him "Rowdy Randy." To prove his point, he resigned his office in the Cabinet, thinking that he would immediately be invited back.

Winston at fifteen looked very natty in his top hat and with a flower in his lapel.

But he had guessed wrong. His resignation was accepted. His own party was tired of "Rowdy Randy." He had to go and sit on the back benches in the House with other members of his party who were out of favor.

However, Lord Randolph remained Winston's hero. He was too young to understand the details, but he was sure everything his father said was right and that everybody else was wrong.

IV. From Toy Soldiers to Sandhurst

As Winston grew older his soldiers weren't toys any more. They had become a hobby.

Whenever he came home from school at Harrow for a holiday, he would spend hours in the old nursery where his soldiers still stood on the long table. Now he studied maps of famous campaigns. He deployed his troops according to plan.

He had well over a thousand soldiers now, and was always getting more. Many of his father's friends were "top brass" in the army. They would come into the nursery with Winston and move the soldiers around and make suggestions. Afterwards they would send him more soldiers and cannon, and models of wagons and caissons. His army grew and grew.

One day his father came into the nursery. Winston was thrilled. The troops were arranged in correct formation for attack. Lord Randolph stood there, studying the little scene, and asking Winston questions. He seemed pleased.

He stayed for about twenty minutes. Just before he left, Lord Randolph asked his son whether he would like to go into the army. Winston said yes.

"My future was settled right then and there," Winston said later.

British officers are trained at a military academy called Sandhurst, very much like the American West Point.

Winston had been enrolled for several years at Harrow, one of the largest and most fashionable boys' schools in England. The whole time he was there he had managed to preserve his standing as low boy in his class. Several times he was on the verge of being dropped. Later in life, he himself said that the reason he was not dropped was because he was the son of the brilliant Lord Randolph Churchill and "therefore couldn't be a complete fool."

But now that it had been decided he was going to Sandhurst, he just had to begin to study for his entrance examinations.

The headmaster of the school began to tutor him privately. Winston soon discovered how foolish he had been to learn only those things that interested him. He just didn't seem to be able to make up for lost time. Twice he took the Sandhurst examinations, and twice he failed them.

Winston thought his Royal Military Academy cadet's uniform was very becoming to him — and so it was.

...ndhurst is the West Point of England where officers of the Queen receive their training.

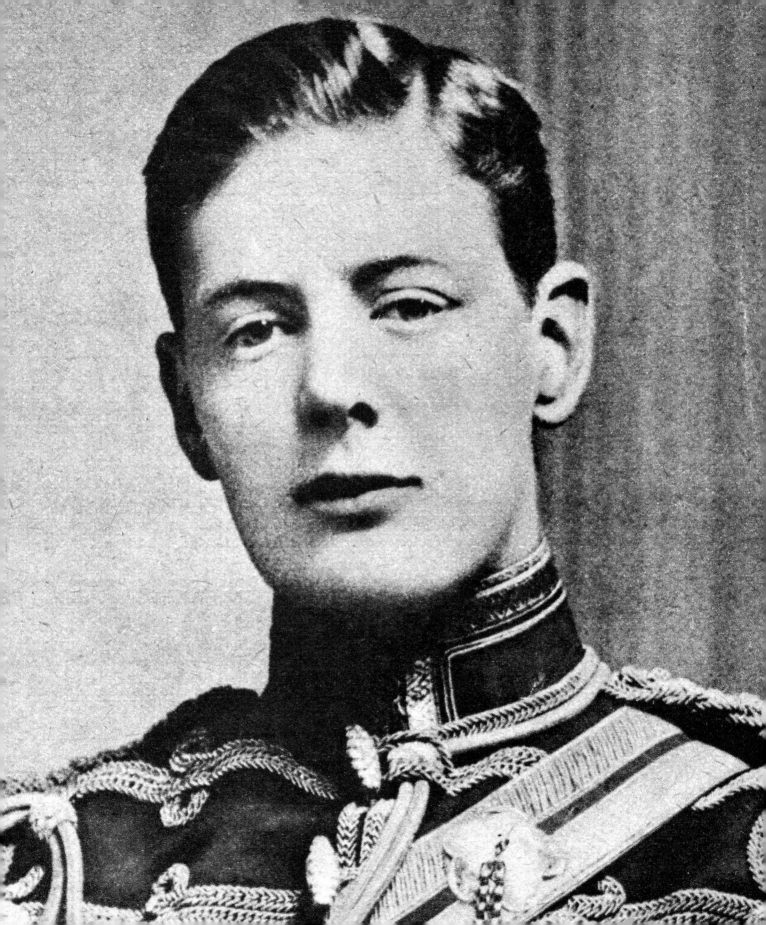

Even in his teens, Winston would not accept failure. He left Harrow and made ready to go to a "cram" school. In this school they had lists of all the questions and answers that had been used in Sandhurst examinations for years. The pupils were required to learn them by rote. It was the kind of thing Winston could do very well. He had often proved that he had a wonderful memory when he wanted to use it.

But before Winston could enroll at the "crammers," he had a serious accident. Because of his injury he was in bed for three months, and it was a full year before he could return to his studies.

It was during this year that Winston came to know more about his father's political career and to take an interest in politics. Once he was out of bed, he went to the House of Commons and listened to the speeches. The Conservatives were no longer in power, and Lord Randolph's acid speeches were now directed against the Liberals.

At home Winston had a chance to meet many of the great men of the day, who came to visit his father and mother. But this kind of good times could not last forever. The year passed, and Winston was well enough to go to the "crammers." In August, 1893, he passed his examination for Sandhurst on the third try. Even so, he didn't get very good grades. He just made the Cavalry School, the lowest division at Sandhurst.

Winston himself was perfectly satisfied to be in the Cavalry. The subjects he had to study just suited him. There were Tactics, Fortifications, Map-Making, Military Law, and Military Administration. This meant that he was studying about the movements of soldiers and the strategy of famous battles. He learned trick riding, and he played polo. He already had fenced in his schooldays at Harrow. The fencing helped him with his saber practice.

He worked hard at Sandhurst, but when he was on leave he went to the theater with his father and to parties given by his mother and her friends. He showed off his uniform and was very witty and gay.

Some people thought he was too brash and forward, but most of them laughed at his jokes. Many of the older and important officers who had seen his collection of soldiers promised to take him into their regiments after he was graduated.

All of this was to help him along in later life.

Winston tried to talk politics to his father. But Lord Randolph just couldn't take him seriously. He still treated his son like a little boy.

The Conservatives were in power again, but Lord Randolph was not invited back into the Cabinet. He had to sit quietly and watch bills come up, many of which he did not approve. If he was allowed to make a speech, no one seemed to pay any attention to what he said. The bills were passed in spite of him.

Being unimportant was more than Lord Randolph could bear. He became ill.

Winston was almost ready to be graduated from Sandhurst. He was doing quite well in his studies. For the first time in his life, he was proving to himself that he was able to do anything he made up his mind to do. He wanted very much to tell his father all about it. He wanted to talk to his father, man to man.

But Lord Randolph died before Winston had a chance.

Winston made a promise to himself that someday he would find a way to make people really appreciate his father.

Soon after, Winston finished at Sandhurst. He was among the first eight in his class. He was assigned to the 4th Hussars. Now he was "in the main the master of my fortunes."

But he was always sad that his father didn't know.

[31]

wenty-one and a subaldern now, Winston wore
e full dress uniform of the 4th Queen's Own
Hussars.

V. Adventure in Cuba

Winston was given a commission. The 4th Hussars was a dandy cavalry regiment with a dashing commander, Colonel Brabazon. Colonel Brabazon had been a friend of Lord Randolph.

Winston rode and drilled afoot with the troopers. He learned to mount and dismount a barebacked horse going at a trot or canter. He jumped bars without stirrups or saddle, sometimes even with his hands clasped behind his back. When he was thrown, he picked himself up and started all over again.

But he loved every minute of it. He loved most of all the excitement of practicing "cavalry charge" and wheeling into formation. He galloped about with drawn saber, shouting to his men.

When Winston's cavalry training was over, he was given a leave. He decided that he would like to see a war. He thought a war would be a fine adventure.

The Spanish Government was trying to put down a rebellion on the island of Cuba. Winston decided to go to Cuba.

He got important letters of introduction to assure himself of a welcome from the Spanish forces in Cuba. He made an arrangement with a London newspaper, the *Daily Graphic,* to send back reports. The paper promised to pay £5 for each.

Then he and another young adventurer took off for Cuba.

The first few days that they were there, they spent following the Spanish troops. Finally they caught up with them in the interior. All the Spaniards seemed to be doing was marching and counter-marching. Winston had the fun of bivouacking in the open. He learned to smoke Havana cigars, drank his rum rations with the men, and took an afternoon nap, or siesta, every day. All these habits Winston kept the rest of his life.

But the fun was soon over. On Winston's twenty-first birthday, the Spaniards flushed out a band of Cuban guerrillas.

"For the first time in my life," Winston wrote his paper, "I saw bullets strike flesh and whistle through the air."

All around him he saw men fall, wounded and dying. He almost was shot himself.

Winston was beginning to wonder whether war was such a fine adventure after all.

Cuban rebels attack Spanish soldiers at LaRosa.

VI. With the Army in India

When Winston returned to England, he received word that his regiment had been ordered to India.

He was delighted to find that his articles in the *Daily Graphic* had made quite a hit. It was nice to have made a reputation as a battle veteran and newspaper man. He noticed that people listened to him more respectfully now when he held forth. He was considered something of an authority on war.

Once Winston was invited to a dinner party where the Prince of Wales was to be present. Being invited to be present at a dinner party for the Prince of Wales was a great honor, and all the guests were supposed to be there before the prince arrived.

But Winston, like his father before him, could not do anything that everybody was expected to do. He was late — more than half an hour late.

When he finally arrived, he was mortified to find that all the dinner guests, including the Prince of Wales, were waiting for him to come. Nobody in the Royal Family would ever sit down to dinner with thirteen at table. Winston had been asked merely to make the fourteenth person.

"Don't they teach you to be punctual in your regiment?" asked the prince in his most severe tone.

"It was an awful moment," Winston said later, telling about it. But after a little while, he said, the prince put him at his ease by "some gracious, chaffing remark."

"I do think unpunctuality is a vile habit, and all my life I have tried to break myself of it," Winston wrote. He admitted that he knew perfectly well how to break himself of the habit. All he had to do was start on time. But he never learned.

"I had all the qualities that made me popular at a gay dinner or a big ball," said Winston, telling about this time of his life. "That is, all except modesty."

But Winston never learned to be very modest. A man who was to become a great leader had to be sure of himself.

The 4th Hussars soon left for India. The regiment was stationed in Bangalore in the south.

Edward Gibbon, one of Winston's inspirations, from a painting by Sir Joshua Reynolds.

Winston was an excellent horseman and made the polo team in Bangalore.

[35]

The Duke of Connaught presents war medals to the 13th Bengal Lancers in India.

With three other young officers, Winston set up housekeeping — in a pink and white bungalow all covered with roses. They engaged a big staff of Indian servants to look after them.

It was really all very pleasant. Of course, mornings were taken up with drill. But after a good lunch and a siesta, they had no more duties. The rest of the day was given to playing polo.

Winston made the regimental polo team.

Time passed. Winston had made a discovery. He noticed that many times when his friends met and discussed serious matters he found that he didn't have the knowledge to join in the talk. He began to be sorry that he had been such a poor student.

So with real Winstonian enthusiasm, he began to educate himself.

He had always liked to read. But now he read serious books as well as stories of adventure. He read instead of taking his siesta. He discovered that Macaulay, who had written his old favorite, *Lays of Ancient Rome,* had also written a five-volume history of England. He got hold of the five volumes and read every one. After Macaulay, he tackled the six volumes of Gibbon's *Decline and Fall of the Roman Empire.* He gobbled them up. He read everything he could get his hands on. His mother sent him more books from England.

But of all the books he read, he liked Macaulay and Gibbon best. He admired the way they used English. He decided to try to write the way they did. He practiced making sentences and using words like his new heroes.

So, at twenty-two, Winston Churchill taught himself to write well-rounded sentences and to use words that counted. He developed a style that stayed with him all the rest of his life. Because of this self-teaching, Churchill's speeches and slogans are exciting to read, and thrilling to quote.

BETTMANN ARCHIVE

[37]

Lord Kitchener and his troops enter Omdurman on the eve of battle.

The months passed. Winston was back in London when border fighting broke out in India. The Head of the Field Force accepted him as a war correspondent.

Up there in the hills, the Pathans, a mountain people, were trying to keep the English from occupying their country. The Pathans had only spears and old-fashioned muskets. But even so, because the country was so mountainous, they were able to hold off the well-armed English troops. The fighting followed a pattern. First the Pathans would ambush English soldiers in a mountain pass and cut them to pieces. Then other English troops would march on a Pathan village and burn it down.

This was the kind of warfare that Winston saw in northern India. He didn't think much of it. He began to have a few doubts about how the English handled colonial affairs. And he also began to question the way the British Army was managed by the officers.

Of course, being Winston, he had to express his ideas. He wrote articles on both subjects for London and Indian papers and magazines. The articles were a great success among his civilian readers, but naturally they didn't make him very popular with army officers and members of the Government.

"Churchill was widely regarded in the Army as insufferably bumptious," said one high-ranking army officer.

Back in Bangalore with his regiment, and once more with nothing much to do except play polo, Winston sat down and wrote two books. One, *The Malakand Field Force,* was published in England and was very successful. The Prince of Wales wrote him a letter of congratulation. But Sir Herbert Kitchener, an important army officer and an old friend of his father, was very much displeased.

The other book, *Savrola,* a novel, was sold as a serial to a magazine. But even Winston had to admit that it wasn't a very good novel.

"I have consistently urged my friends to abstain from reading it," he said when he grew older.

And so, between reading and writing, polo playing and arguing, the time passed.

Winston had earned himself a four-months' leave from India. He determined to go adventuring again.

In April, 1876, Queen Victoria was declared Empress of India, a title many considered to be "un-English."

VII. Up the Nile

Egypt was in a turmoil. The Pasha of Egypt was not only the king but also the religious head of the country. Everybody was supposed to obey him without question. But the reigning pasha was weak and lazy, so the real rulers of the country were the Dervishes, a fanatical religious sect, fierce and warlike.

The peasants of Egypt — the fellahin — were very poor. They lived in daily terror of the Dervishes. They knew they had to do whatever the Dervishes wanted. Otherwise, a mounted band on magnificent Arabian horses, brandishing knives, shouting and shooting off their muskets, would gallop into the village, take everything there was to take, slash down everybody who opposed them, and carry off the women and children.

Just before Winston was born, the English had made a bargain with the grandfather of the reigning pasha. They paid him a big sum of money. In return, he gave them control of the Suez Canal, and the English promised to keep peace in Egypt.

Of course, the Dervishes didn't like this. They tried to drive the British out of Egypt. But the hard-riding, shouting Dervishes had only knives and swords and old-fashioned muskets with which to fight the well-trained British troops with their modern guns and cannon. Instead of chasing the British, the British chased them.

The British chased the Dervishes farther and farther away from the Canal, up beyond Aswan, out of Egypt, eight hundred miles up the Nile and into the Sudan.

In the Sudan, the Dervishes holed up in their capital, Omdurman.

The British were determined to wipe out the Dervishes. They sent twenty thousand men, under Sir Herbert Kitchener, to Egypt. With the

Outside Cairo stands Egypt's ancient Sphinx.

[41]

troops went a fleet of gunboats, carrying supplies and cannon. Men and boats began moving up the Nile together to storm Omdurman.

Winston made up his mind to go to Egypt and see what was going on. He easily got orders from several papers and magazines for articles. This time he was to be paid $45.00 for each article. He was coming up as a writer.

But it wasn't so easy to get permission to go with the British Army. Sir Herbert Kitchener hadn't forgotten what Winston had written from India and refused to have him come along.

This didn't stop Winston. Once he had made up his mind to do something, he was going to do it. He managed to get an appointment to a unit that was not under Sir Herbert. And then he took off for Egypt.

Winston caught up with the main army before they had reached Omdurman. As the great British force drew nearer and nearer to Omdurman, reports came in of hordes of Dervishes all dressed in white, mounted on horses, and drawn up in battle array, waiting to cut the British to pieces.

But once the battle was drawn, the Dervishes

Winston took part in the last classic cavalry charge in the history of war, at Omdurman.

had no real chance. Shouting and waving their spears and muskets, they charged the British line. They were met with a deadly barrage from up-to-date rifles and modern cannon. The Dervishes kept right on coming. Charge after charge was mowed down. The plains were strewn with dead bodies.

They had taken an oath to win or die, and so they died.

Winston's reports of the Dervish Charge were sensational. He described every detail. One story, in which he wrote about finding a Dervish mother

The Camel Corps of the British Army.

and child among the slain warriors, was talked about wherever English was read. And soon, of course, he wrote a book about his experiences, *The River War*.

But Winston gained more in the Egyptian campaign than just a reputation as an exceptional writer.

Just before the battle was joined, Winston, at great risk, went out ahead of the troops, in a scouting party. He brought back an important report of the position of the Dervish horde. He delivered the report personally to Sir Herbert Kitchener.

Sir Herbert swiftly acted on the report. But he gave no sign of recognition to the messenger. Years later, however, Winston and Kitchener worked side by side as equals.

VIII. South African Adventure

The British Army moved into Omdurman, and Winston made ready to return to his regiment.

Winston was now twenty-five. Looking back, he realized that his two books and his articles had brought in nearly five times as much as he had earned in three years in the army. And, as a writer, he didn't have to buy expensive uniforms and keep a string of polo ponies.

So Winston decided to leave the army. First he had to return to India to resign from his regiment. He stayed just long enough to help win an important polo match. Then he went back home.

Since he was a celebrity, the Conservative Party invited him to stand for a seat in Parliament from the Borough of Oldham.

Winston went to Oldham, a mill town, to campaign. But he had been away from England so long that he didn't know how to talk to the voters about the things that they wanted to know. He was roundly beaten. Winston accepted his defeat, but privately he made up his mind that some day he would make up for it.

With his usual luck, his next venture was to help him do just that.

During the previous hundred and fifty years, the Dutch had been going to live in South Africa. They broke the ground. Then the English came.

Both colonies grew bigger and bigger. As they went farther into the interior of Africa, they began to get in each other's way. To add to the difficulty, diamonds and gold were discovered. The Dutch settlers — the Boers — and the English began to argue about who owned which part of the country. Of course, neither of them paid any attention to the fact that the country really belonged to the African tribes who were already living there.

Arguments between the colonists became hotter. The neighbors began shooting at each other.

The Boers had set up two independent nations in South Africa. But the English who lived there were still British subjects. They expected their mother country to help them.

England found herself with a real war on her hands. This was no minor campaign against Pathans with spears or Dervishes on horseback. The

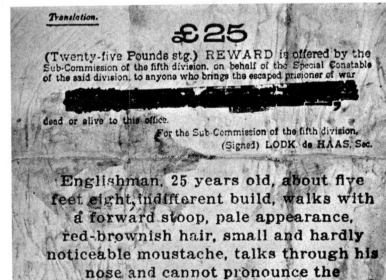

The pin-up boy of his day — Winston in 1901 during the Boer War.

[45]

Boers were determined to preserve their independence. They were great fighters, even with pitchforks, and they knew every inch of the bush. For a number of years they held the British off. It looked at first as though they would win.

At last England sent reinforcements. Along with the reinforcements went Winston, as a newspaper correspondent for the *Morning Post*. He at once managed to get to where the fighting was thickest. He fearlessly volunteered to join a scouting party on an armored train, which was to try to penetrate into the bush, where bands of Boer sharpshooters were lying in wait. The armored train hadn't gone very far when it ran into a Boer ambush. Winston jumped out of the train. Dodging a hail of enemy bullets, he directed the escape of the train. Because of Winston's bravery and cool-headedness, only a handful of British were captured.

Winston tried to make a getaway through the bush, but before long he found himself face to face with a big, bearded Boer farmer with a gun.

Winston managed to get rid of his pistol just before the Boer cornered him. Then he explained that he was a war correspondent. Winston was a fast talker, but the big man just laughed. Everybody recognized the red-haired, freckled young man who had bravely directed the escape of the train.

So Winston was sent with the captured British to a prison in Pretoria. Pretoria was the Boer capital up north and far away from where the fighting was going on.

Three years later, Winston met his Boer captor again. His name was Louis Botha. He was to become the Prime Minister of the South African Republic, and to lead the united forces of English and Boers against the Germans in Africa. He became as valuable a friend as he had been a brave enemy.

Winston is on the extreme right among other

Winston was no sooner in prison in Pretoria than he began to look around for ways to escape. He conspired with several English officers in an elaborate plan of escape. But he was the only one able to carry it through.

He escaped from the prison under the very noses of his guards. Then he walked right through the city to the railroad station without attracting

Winston wasn't discouraged. He climbed out of his hiding place and started walking east. He kept on walking most of the night. At last he came to a house. He was so hungry that he decided to take a chance. He rapped on the door.

What luck! The owner of the house was an Englishman! With the help of another Englishman, a mining engineer named Dewsnap, from Oldham, he hid Winston at the bottom of the mine. A few days later, he packed Winston, well supplied with food, in the bottom of a railway car loaded with sheepskins.

Now Winston was really on his way to freedom. At Lourenço Marques, on the east coast, he was sure he could get a ship back to the British port of Durban in South Africa.

Winston's escape had been widely reported. There were pieces in the papers. The Boers offered a reward for him of $100.00. When nobody turned him in, he was given up for lost. So when he landed in Durban, he was given a tremendous reception. The story of his bravery in the ambush of the armored train was known everywhere. He was a hero, and was carried through the city cheered by great crowds of people.

Winston stayed with the British for two more campaigns. His courage and his escape had made him famous. His dispatches to the papers added to his fame.

When he went back to England, he found that there, too, he was a hero.

prisoners of the Boers, in November 1889.

any notice. He hid in a freight car and when the train began to move, he went to sleep.

Hours later he awoke. He peeped out and found he was out in the middle of the bush.

Winston had studied the geography of the country. He knew there was a Portuguese colony to the east, and if he could get there he would be safe. But it was three hundred miles away.

BETTMANN ARCHIVE
Winston was photographed after his escape from the Boers, on December 12, 1899

IX. Brash Backbencher

When Winston Churchill made up his mind to do something, he never gave up.

He couldn't forget that he had tried for Parliament from Oldham and had been beaten there. So, when the Conservative Party asked him to try Oldham again, he jumped at the chance.

Of course, it would cost him money. Campaigns were expensive, and Members of Parliament still were not paid salaries. But by this time Winston was sure that he could make a good living writing and lecturing.

This time when Winston went to Oldham to speak, the whole audience stood up and cheered before he said a word. Mr. Dewsnap, the man who had helped him hide in the mine during his escape from Pretoria, had written his wife all about it. Mrs. Dewsnap went around everywhere with Winston, helping him win votes.

Winston's campaign was known as "the khaki election." He was such a success as a speaker that even the most important Conservatives drafted him to make speeches for them too. Winston won by two hundred and thirty votes.

"Was it wonderful that I should have thought I had arrived?" Winston said when he grew older. "But luckily life is not so easy as all that: otherwise, we should get to the end too quickly."

Before Winston took his seat in Parliament, he went lecturing. He traveled all over England and Canada and the United States. He was wined and dined by famous people everywhere. Even Mark Twain was glad to meet him in America.

And why not! Winston's jaunty picture as the Boer War correspondent was all over the country. He was the "pin-up" boy of the period.

While Winston was still in America, Queen Victoria died. So he missed the great funeral procession through the streets of London in which

The Houses of Parliament seen from across the river Thames.

[49]

five kings and forty members of royal families marched.

Queen Victoria had been related to almost all the crowned heads of Europe. She had married her cousin. He also was related to kings and princes. Many of their nine children had married royalty.

During the sixty-four years of Queen Victoria's reign, at some time or other all these cousins and nephews and aunts and uncles and sons-in-law and daughters-in-law and grandchildren had come to visit her in England.

Queen Victoria always spoke her mind. She would tell her guests plainly how they ought to run their countries. She was a great letter writer, too. In between visits, she would write and give them more instructions.

In this way Queen Victoria was the real boss of Europe. Everybody was a little afraid of her. This made England very powerful among the European nations.

Queen Victoria did not trust her oldest son, Albert Edward, the Prince of Wales, to handle government matters. She thought he was a "playboy." Most of his royal relatives agreed with her.

When Victoria died, the Prince of Wales was proclaimed Edward VII, King of England. Fortunately, Victoria had misjudged her son. He was much more capable than she had believed he was.

The new king opened Parliament in February, 1901. Winston had made a good deal of money with his lectures. He now felt free to give his time to politics. He was very much excited when he went the first day to the Houses of Parliament to take his place in the Commons. He felt that, at twenty-six, he had arrived at a red-letter day in his career. Although he was already a celebrity, actually, as a new M.P., his presence was not considered very important. His seat in the House of Commons was in the last row on the Conservative Party side. He was a "backbencher."

Backbenchers were just supposed to vote "Aye" or "Nay" with their party. They weren't expected to do much talking.

But Winston had no intention of being ignored. That wasn't his style. Before three days had passed, he arranged to be asked to make a speech.

The House was crowded, and so was the Visitors' Gallery. People were anxious to find out what kind of a speech "Rowdy Randy's" son would make.

Winston surprised them. Instead of being a fire-eater, he spoke with the greatest conservatism. He closed his speech by thanking the House for the kindness, courtesy, and patience with which the Members had listened to him.

"It has been extended to me, I know," he said, "not on my own account but because of a splendid memory which many Honorable Members still preserve."

As soon as Winston went outside of the chamber into the corridor, people crowded around him to congratulate him. His speech was well written, well delivered, and moderate, was the general opinion.

Winston had come off with flying colors.

From then on, whenever it became known that Winston was to make a speech — and he managed to make many more than most backbenchers — the House was crowded.

Winston himself wasn't too surprised by his success. He was used to enthusiastic audiences at his lectures. He had evolved a system of speech writing. He would put down every word beforehand. Then he would polish and repolish his sentences until he thought they were well rounded and balanced. He tried to make them sound as Macaulay or Gibbon would have written them.

Once he was satisfied with the writing, he

A reception is held on the terrac
outside the House of Parliamen

would begin working on his delivery, standing in front of a mirror watching himself and reciting his speech over and over again until he had memorized both it and the gestures that went with it. He had this down to such a fine art that when he actually delivered the speech he sounded as though he were making it up as he went along.

But just making successful speeches was not enough for Winston. His goal was to become important in his party and be appointed to the Cabinet where policies were made.

The older and more successful leaders in the Conservative Party were not anxious to give up their places to younger men. They were cool to the brash young backbencher who spoke his mind so often, even though they were entertained by his acid wit.

He began making enemies. People started to remark that what he had to say wasn't as important as the way he said it. He wasn't sincere, they said, he was just a clever actor. *Punch,* the great political comic weekly, ran a cartoon of him choosing a role and then taking lessons in putting it over from the popular star, Henry Irving.

As a matter of fact, Winston was not being very original. At first, he modeled all his ideas on those of his father.

He began writing *The Life of Lord Randolph Churchill.* The more he studied his father's ideas, the more he came to believe in them. And since many of his father's ideas had been opposed to those of his party, Winston found himself disagreeing more and more with the Conservatives. He didn't hesitate to express his dissatisfaction whenever he spoke or wrote.

He realized that his ideas about the reconstruction of South Africa were more like those of the party of the Opposition — the Liberal Party. Little by little, it seemed that he was getting ready to change parties.

Winston's slogan, he said, was "In war, resolution. In defeat, defiance. In victory, magnanimity. In peace, good will."

He had been three years in Commons when he rose and made a decisive speech against an important bill. At the end of his speech, he stalked across the aisle and dramatically took a seat on the Liberal side.

X. A New Party and A New Partner

The Opposition received Winston with open arms. Now, when he made biting speeches, he added to the importance of the Liberal Party.

Actually Winston didn't fit well into any party system. He joined the Liberals, partly because he admired their leader, David Lloyd George, and partly because there he got plenty of opportunity to speak. And there was no other important party for him to join.

In 1908, when an election came up, the Liberals offered Winston a chance to contest Northwest Manchester.

Northwest Manchester certainly was not a good choice since it had long been a Conservative town. In addition, it was the home of Mrs. Emmeline Pankhurst and her two daughters, Cristabel and Sylvia. Mrs. Pankhurst was the leader of a large group — the Suffragettes — who were trying to get a Bill through Parliament to allow women to vote.

Winston didn't see any reason why women should not vote. But Mrs. Pankhurst demanded the support of the Prime Minister, which Winston couldn't promise. So Mrs. Pankhurst and her followers followed Winston everywhere, and when he spoke they broke up the meetings.

Winston couldn't win in Northwest Manchester. The Conservatives were delighted. They considered Winston their number one enemy.

In the dark days ahead Winston and Lloyd George were to work tirelessly together.

[53]

But the Liberals were not willing to let Winston lose. They sent him to Dundee, a "safe" Liberal stronghold in Scotland, where he found the Suffragettes' heckling less of a problem.

This was probably the luckiest thing that ever happened to Winston. For one of the people who worked on his campaign in Dundee was Miss Clementine Hozier.

Miss Hozier was everything that Winston admired — beautiful, lively, a great reader, and interested in politics. For the first time in his life, Winston fell in love.

In 1910 many English suffragettes were arrested for disorderly conduct.

On September 12, 1908, Clementine Hozier and Winston Churchill were married.

Miss Hozier went campaigning with him all over the district. As soon as he had won his seat, they were married, and as Winston said, "they lived happily ever afterwards."

Their wedding was one of the great social events of the season. For though Miss Hozier was a true Liberal and cared very little about whether people were earls and dukes and princes unless she was fond of them personally, Winston, after all, was a public figure, a popular lecturer and a well-known writer. Not only did members of his own party come to the wedding, but men who were supposed to be his bitterest political enemies came as well.

But after the wedding, practically nobody "in society" would sit down to dinner with him. He had walked out of the Conservative Party, and he was a social outcast. The only fashionable house where he was welcome was Blenheim, where his cousin was now the Duke of Marlborough.

But the new Mrs. Churchill did not seem to care a bit. As a matter of fact, she seemed to prefer the company of forward-looking persons to the hard-shell Conservatives whom she considered a wee bit stuffy. Before long, she had made quite a circle of her own, where there was plenty of good talk about literature and art and music, and above all, about politics.

It was fortunate that the new Mrs. Churchill was interested in politics, for Winston was on his way up.

The Liberals were in the saddle. The new Prime Minister was a Liberal. He appreciated Winston's ability and gave him Cabinet appointments. These appointments did not put Winston into the inner circle of policy-making Cabinet members, but they gave him the chance to work his way up gradually in the Liberal Party.

The first of Winston's appointments was that of Under-Secretary of State for the Colonies. He was fortunate to hold that position at a time when the Boer War ended, and the question of the reconstruction of the territories Britain had won was being discussed in the Colonial Office. Winston was delighted to be able to take part in the proceedings which in the end resulted in the creation of the Union of South Africa.

Winston's next job was that of Home Secretary. Although, as always, he was efficient and administered his office well, he was not so fortunate in the policies he pursued.

When the Welsh miners, who were among the poorest paid of all the workers in England, struck for higher wages and better working conditions, Winston sent first the police and then the military to deal with the miners. This action called down great criticism on the Home Secretary and on the Liberal Party. For most of the public sympathy was with the miners. But Winston, at that time, because of his training and temperament, regarded any disorderly strike as a threat to public safety rather than as a social right. And therefore that was the way he dealt with it.

He was much more modern in his attitude toward other things. He introduced many reforms into the English prison system and did away with many of the harsh measures which should have been abolished long before.

A great change had begun in the early part of the nineteenth century and was just becoming a political force while Winston was Home Secretary. During this time, England had been changing from being mainly an agricultural country into one of the greatest industrial countries in the world.

This change had been brought about first of all by the invention of the steam engine and its introduction for use in factories and mills and mines. People who had lived on farms or worked in local industries crowded into the cities where the big factories were and went to work there. So many of them came to the cities that the employers could pay them the smallest wages.

Besides this, the type of workers needed in the factory was so unskilled that even children could do the jobs. Boys and girls seven or eight or nine years old could do the work of a grown man. Whole families went into the mills and the mines, working from sunup to sundown and hardly making enough money to feed and clothe themselves properly.

This great period of change in living is sometimes called the Industrial Revolution. It was the beginning of what we now call Automation.

At first this new way of life was hailed by most people as a great gain. England became very prosperous.

But by and by, thoughtful people began to notice that though the rich were becoming richer, the poor were becoming poorer. They began calling attention to the fact that men who were making fortunes in manufacturing, and promoting railroads and canals and big businesses, were living better and better, but thousands of factory workers were spending their lives without ever seeing the sun, and thousands of children were growing up without proper food and without any schooling at all.

Toward the middle of the nineteenth century a German, Karl Marx, who was living in exile in London and writing articles for the *New York Tribune*, predicted that before long the workers would rise in revolt against their lot and introduce a new form of government into England.

Marx was wrong, of course, for the English way of improving things is by legislation. A

Karl Marx's last works, Das Kapital, *was completed by his collaborator.*

Shaw made sharp, witty attacks on the politics of Britain.

Wells was outspoken in his criticism of English life of his day.

group of brilliant writers and reformers put themselves at the head of a movement to get better conditions for the industrial workers through Parliamentary action.

In 1910, when Winston became Home Secretary, this group had a very large following indeed among the British voters. They were so strong that they had forced the Liberal Party to adopt their ideas for social reform.

Among these leaders were the well-known and distinguished writers, H. G. Wells and George Bernard Shaw.

Both Shaw and Wells were friends of Mrs. Churchill, and Winston often saw them in his own home. But he knew very little about the "depressed classes" from actual experience. And his real interest was in foreign and not domestic affairs.

Winston's next job was that of President of the Board of Trade. This position in some ways corresponds to that of the American Secretary of Commerce. Winston was not too happy in having his work entirely among business people. But no matter what his duties were, he had his own ideas about everything. He was always writing long letters to other members of the Cabinet telling them how to manage their own departments. He could not understand why they didn't like his doing this.

Many of the other Cabinet members thought "Winnie" had better mind his own business. "One might as well try to rebuke a brass band," one Cabinet member complained.

Winston had, by now, proved his usefulness to the Liberal Party. At last he was appointed First Lord of the Admiralty, an appointment which really suited his talents. Now he would take part in the shaping of international policy.

*Winston probably set his watch by Big Ben man—
a time on his way to the House of Common—*

XI. Danger Ahead

Even before Winston became First Lord of the Admiralty, many of his notes to the members of the Cabinet had been about Germany, and so were his public speeches.

The great powers of Europe had been at peace with each other since the end of the Franco-Prussian War in 1871. This peace was called *Pax Britannica* (The British Peace). It was largely the result of the great might of England. England was the greatest colonial power in the world, the most prosperous and the most important, and her people the best governed of any country in Europe. In addition, she had a large military establishment and the finest navy afloat.

Britain was a commercial country. Her prosperity depended on peaceful exchange between the British Isles and her colonies, and with the countries all over the world with whom she traded. The British Navy was chiefly occupied in maintaining this peaceful exchange. In a way, it was doing police duty to preserve what we could call today the Freedom of the Seas.

Winston was suspicious of Germany. He had traveled in Germany. He had heard Prussian officers and street crowds singing *"Deutschland Uber Alles."* He was sure that Germany was ambitious to take the place of Britain as the number one world power. He thought that Germany's objective would be, not peace like England's, but war. He had heard talk of *Der Tag* (The Day). By *Der Tag,* the Germans meant that day when they would prove their superiority by some military coup, probably against their ancient enemy, France.

Many people pooh-poohed this talk. But it was no secret that Germany was building the biggest battleships in the world. What would they want those big battleships for, Winston reasoned? Except to use them against the British Navy on *Der Tag.*

Winston had long kept his eye on Kaiser Wilhelm.

Winston's ideas about Germany had been shared by his friend, King Edward VII.

Edward's oldest sister, Victoria Adelaide Mary Louise, had married the King of Prussia, who was also the Emperor of Germany, Frederick III. Edward was very fond of his sister Vicki, and Vicki was devoted to her brother Bertie.

When Frederick died, he was succeeded by his son, William II. The new Kaiser Wilhelm was conceited and opinionated. He was fond of putting on fancy uniforms and strutting around and showing off. Bertie didn't like his nephew. He thought Wilhelm did not treat his mother with proper respect and kindness. Wilhelm didn't like Uncle Bertie very much either. No matter how hard Wilhelm tried, he could not cut as big a dash in international society as his English uncle could. Edward VII was the idol of the Parisians. But the French disliked everything German, and they disliked the German Kaiser most of all.

Wilhelm tried to outshine his uncle at the Cowes regatta. He came there on a yacht far more luxurious and ornate than that of the English king. But even this didn't make him popular with the yachting set.

Wilhelm was very angry, and he didn't hesitate to say so publicly like a spoiled little boy. He rather looked down on the English kings where the sovereign was directly responsible to the Parliament elected by the people, and the laws were made by the people's representatives and not by the king.

The German emperors, like the sovereigns of the Middle Ages, ruled their people by "divine right." That is, they believed they had been selected to govern their subjects by God Himself. Very often the Kaiser used the expression, *"Ich und Gott,"* ("I and God"), and he acted as though he believed it.

By the time Winston became First Lord of the Admiralty, Edward's son, George V, was king. The new king was not like his father. George was quiet and home-loving and didn't understand the ways of the world.

King George V and Queen Mary pay their first state visit to the City of London on the day after their coronation in 1911

He believed that everybody really wanted peace. This included Germany.

Winston had reason to believe that Wilhelm was trying to make a deal with Tsar Nicholas of Russia to stay neutral in case Germany went to war with France. Years later, the whole correspondence between the two rulers was discovered. They had addressed each other affectionately as "Willi" and "Nicky," and they had plans for conquering the world. The letters became known as the "Willi-Nicky letters." But even while "Willi" was writing these letters, he was also having dealings with Russia's enemies in Turkey and in the Balkans. When "Nicky" discovered this, he made a treaty with England for mutual defense.

The Kaiser also threatened to undermine France's influence in her North African colonies. He sent a fleet to Morocco, but before anything happened, Winston sent an even bigger English fleet into the Mediterranean and the Germans backed down.

Even with all these things going on, Winston wasn't able to convince anybody, in the government or out, that Germany was getting ready for war. So, on his own, without encouragement from anybody, he went ahead and used his new position of power, as First Lord of the Admiralty, to strengthen the British Navy.

The Kaiser was furious and said so, but Winston didn't care a bit about what the Kaiser thought of him. He remembered the pillow fight they had had at a weekend party when Wilhelm was visiting in England. Winston hadn't liked him even then. The Kaiser returned the compliment. He thought Winston was stupid. Both men made belligerent speeches.

Winston spent his first six months as First Lord of the Admiralty visiting every single warship and installation of the British Navy. He cruised all over the Empire. He learned the size of every gun,

Tsar Nicholas reviews a Russian infantry regiment during the Russo-Japanese War.

the number of guns, the number of men, how they lived, how they were fed, and what they wore. He got a line on every admiral, captain, boatswain, and even the common sailors.

Then he persuaded Admiral Lord John Fisher, Retired, his father's old friend, to come back into active duty as his adviser. Together, the two men had the navy converted from coal to oil, and mounted the ships with guns of heavier firing power than ever before had been used.

Lord Fisher was even more positive than Winston that Germany was getting ready for war. He even pinned down the date. *Der Tag* would come, he predicted, during the month of July or at the very latest, August 11, in the year 1914.

Time was growing short. Winston could get

The assassin of Grand Duke Ferdinand, heir to Austria's throne, is arrested at Sarajevo, 1914.

no help from his friend, David Lloyd George. Lloyd George agreed with the king about peace, and he was much too busy trying to reform the House of Lords and push through laws in Commons to help the British workmen.

There were hard times in Britain.

The Suffragettes were making more trouble than ever. The miners' strike was put down by the military, but afterwards there was a general strike. When that was settled, there was a railway strike.

Ireland was on the brink of civil war. The Ulsterites in the north of Ireland were getting ready to fight the Sinn Feiners in the south of Ireland. The Ulsterites wanted to remain a part of Britain — or the United Kingdom, as it was coming to be called. The Sinn Feiners still wanted Home Rule.

Winston received word that Germany was shipping guns and ammunition to the Ulsterites. Nothing would make Germany happier, Winston reasoned, than to have England with a civil war on her hands when *Der Tag* came. He talked about it to everyone, but nobody would listen. The British could think only about their own troubles.

On June 23, 1914, at Sarajevo in the Balkans, the Archduke Franz Ferdinand of Austria, heir to the throne, was assassinated by a young student, a member of a patriotic secret society.

On July 28, Austria declared war on Serbia.

Russia, Serbia's ally, mobilized her armies.

Three days later, Germany, Austria's friend, declared war on Russia.

France and Russia had a defensive treaty. So, without warning, the German armies went marching through little Belgium on their way to France.

Der Tag had arrived.

The conquering Germans march through occupied Brussels in August, 1914.

XII. World War I - First Lord

Der Tag came as a horrid surprise to most of the English people.

A few weeks before, when the European powers had began mobilizing, the British Government had half-heartedly brought up the subject of strengthening the military. But practically nothing had been accomplished. The United Kingdom was unprepared for war.

Only the Navy was ready.

The First Lord of the Admiralty believed in Lord Fisher's timetable. July, 1914, came nearer and nearer.

In July, a grand review of the fleet was held. At Spithead Channel, off the southern coast of England, the great ships passed before their king in full battle array.

Secretly, Winston ordered the warships to battle stations.

The moment that Austria attacked Serbia, Winston gave orders for the fleet to proceed to Scapa Flow, a protected sound in the Orkney Islands to the very north of Scotland. From here they would be able to watch every move of the German Navy.

The passage of the fleet through the Straits of Dover and up the North Sea — where only a few miles away a German naval force lay off the entrance to the Kiel Canal — was undertaken in the greatest secrecy. At night the fires on all the ships were banked and the lights put out.

The main body of the fleet reached Scapa Flow at daylight. Then and only then did Winston reveal what he had done and obtain official permission to do it.

Out into the Atlantic steamed another fleet of ships to meet the submarine threat.

Hundreds of less battleworthy craft quickly gathered at English ports ready to carry British troops across the Channel to where the French were fighting desperately to stem the German tide sweeping through Belgium.

On August 4, England declared war on Germany. The British Navy was ready. Her largest warships had their stations in a spot from which they could move freely against the German fleet,

Strolling with John Morley. From 1911 to 1915 Winston was First Lord of the Admiralty.

To encourage enlistment, a volunteer infantry regiment parades through London.

and her remaining tonnage stood ready at Portsmouth to transport the British troops across the Channel to Dunkirk to reinforce the French.

Winston's headlong, impatient habits had paid off. He was the hero of the hour.

Winston's Grand Fleet sailed up and down the North Sea daring the German Navy to come out and fight. His Atlantic fleet went submarine chasing, sinking the undersea boats (U-boats) wherever they could find them. In the Mediterranean, in the Red Sea, and in the Indian Ocean, other British ships ran down German raiders attacking British merchantmen.

At the same time hundreds of smaller boats went scurrying back and forth across the English Channel to France, landing British troops, bringing back the wounded, and carrying supplies to reinforce the hard-pressed French and Belgians.

Winston was not satisfied to have only ships. He had scraped together a few rickety airplanes and set up a Naval Air Service.

Lord Kitchener was War Minister. At last, the two men were serving together. Winston asked that he be allowed to try out his little planes at Dunkirk, where the British forces were getting the worst of it. But at Dunkirk, the airplanes were not able to prevent a British retreat.

Most people didn't think very well of airplanes in those days. But Winston was convinced that future wars would be fought in the air.

Later, he had a real chance to prove the importance of airplanes. His wobbly little planes swept over German zeppelin bases, and before a year was up had destroyed six of the great gas-filled German airships.

The war was going very badly for the Allies. The Belgian Army gave up. The British and French had to pull back to the French border. Winston ordered marines loaded onto gunboats and taken up the river Scheld, to Antwerp. He himself joined them there. After five days, Antwerp fell to the Germans. But Winston's delaying action saved the channel ports.

People were beginning to wonder why the First

Winston saw very early the potential might of an air force in wartime.

Over the top — British infantry ready to go, in the Battle of the Somme.

Lord of the Admiralty didn't attend to his own department and let the generals manage land operations.

Winston *was* attending to his own department. His navy was getting along very well. His Grand Fleet in the North Sea finally forced the Germans to come out and fight, and managed to sink one of the Kaiser's big, new battleships.

Winston was always working. He would work on one project, and after he got that rolling, he would put it aside, and take up another. But he didn't forget the first one.

He always knew exactly where to find each idea when he needed it again. He stored ideas the way other people store books. And in Winston's brain was a whole library of ideas.

This was very irritating to people with one-track minds. But it was one of the things that made Winston a genius.

He began thinking about some kind of battleship which could navigate on land. He ordered two of them to be built. The "land battleships"

were constructed on top of two ordinary steam rollers "fastened together side by side by very strong steel connections." But they were so heavy, they just could not move.

During the second year of the war, both sides began building long trenches. The opposing armies dug themselves in and settled down to trench warfare.

Months passed. The war in France was bogged down in the trenches. Neither side made any great gains on the Western Front.

Winston had been working on his land battleships. Now he was planning to have them move on caterpillars instead of rollers. He was positive that they could break the stalemate.

"The object of these battleships," he told the generals, "is for them to run along the lines of trenches, crushing them flat and burying the people in them."

He came up with a new plan. Why not strike at the enemy's back?

The Dardanelles is a narrow strait that divides

the Continent of Europe from Asia Minor. The Turks, who were Germany's allies, had built strong fortifications on both sides of the Dardanelles.

Winston proposed that a British fleet should sail from the Adriatic Sea into the Dardanelles, and shell the Turkish forts from the water side. At the same time, a small British force should march from Greece into Turkey behind the forts, and attack from the land side. In this way, the forts would be surrounded. Constantinople, the Turkish capital, would be threatened.

This would create a new front. It might make Germany draw off some of her soldiers from the Western Front, and send them to Turkey to help her ally.

Winston was sure that by the time the Germans arrived, the combined British forces would have mopped up the Turks. Then without much opposition, the back door of Germany could be forced.

With the Dardanelles and Constantinople in Allied hands, contact could then be made with the hard-pressed Russians.

The members of the British War Cabinet were not very enthusiastic about Winston's plan. But nobody came up with a better one. So, half-heartedly, they agreed to start the Dardanelles campaign.

Winston didn't delay. His ships went sailing into the Dardanelles and started their bombardment of the Turkish forts. But the military leaders did not work as quickly as Winston. The orders had gone out. The English troops were on their way, but they hadn't arrived yet.

After three days of cannonading, there was still no sign of the military. The fleet withdrew into the Adriatic.

Later, a small British force arrived.

The Turks had only one enemy to fight. They fell upon the British, and cut them to pieces.

The English attempt to land on Gallipoli, August, 1915.

German submarine sinking an armed fishery steamer in the North Sea. BETTMANN ARCHIVE

Only a few escaped. The Dardanelles campaign was a disaster.

News of the slaughter reached England. Everybody blamed Winston Churchill. Why hadn't he waited for the Army? Why was he always trying to run everything? What was such a lone wolf doing in the government anyway?

Things were made even worse by the behavior of Lord Fisher. Lord Fisher wrote a letter, which was made public, denying responsibility for the whole fiasco.

He had not been in favor of the Dardanelles campaign, he said. He had tried to prevent Winston from starting it. He had explained that the most important work for the Navy was to seek an engagement with the main German fleet in the North Sea. He had argued with Winston, he said. But Winston had gone ahead anyway. Now, either Winston must go, or he would go.

Winston tried to persuade Lord Fisher to reconsider, but it was too late. The naval expert was furious with the upstart civilian who had dared to override him.

Winston was forced to resign from the Cabinet. He was no longer First Lord of the Admiralty.

For two years, Winston had been one of the most powerful men in England. Now, suddenly, he had lost his power. Now he was nothing but a "backbencher" again.

Winston's faith in his "land battleships" would someday be justified. Here he is inspecting the 1927 models.

XIII. Between Two Wars

The war dragged on. Winston tried first one job and then another.

He went to France and fought in the trenches. He managed to get into several actions and had a few narrow escapes. But trench warfare didn't give him enough to do.

After a few months in France, he went back home and took his seat in Parliament. From the back benches he fussed and fumed and wrote letters to the Ministers. Nobody listened to him.

Winston had been at loose ends for about a year when his friend, Lloyd George, became Prime Minister. Lloyd George offered Winston the position of Minister of Munitions.

The appointment met with a great deal of opposition. But Lloyd George stood firm. He needed a good organizer in that position, he said. And everybody knew from experience that Winston was a magnificent organizer. Besides, the position of Minister of Munitions did not put Winston in the War Cabinet, where he would have had a hand in policy making.

. As an organizer, Winston lived up to everything Lloyd George expected of him. But he also took out some of his old ideas and dusted them off and experimented with them. His land battleships already had been put into production, and had proved that they could become useful.

Experiments were carried on in the deepest secrecy. Later in the war, some of these "tanks" as they were then called, were sent into action at the Battle of the Somme. The sudden appearance of these moving monsters spread terror among the Germans and broke the line of the trenches, just as Winston had predicted, but nobody seemed to remember his prediction.

Airplanes already had proved themselves. Now he was able to step up plane production for the army-air arm.

When the United States came into the war,

David Lloyd George was once described as the "Prime Minister of Europe."

After a farewell speech to the House of Commons, Winston, now a major in the Oxfordshire Yeomanry, left for France.

in 1917, the Americans were as little ready for a great war as the British had been in 1914. If they were to be properly equipped, they would have to get their arms and ammunition from their allies.

Under Winston's driving force, the factory workers of Britain turned out all the guns and cannon and ammunition that were needed. The Americans recognized his great service, and he was presented with a citation by the American Expeditionary Forces Commander, General Pershing.

But nothing could make Winston forget that he was no longer a key figure in the conduct of the war.

Nor when the war was won was he allowed to help make the peace. Lloyd George did not invite Winston to the Peace Conference in France. Instead he gave him another organizing job at home. He made him Minister of War.

It was the duty of the War Ministry to demobilize the thousands of Britons who had enlisted during the fighting, and return them to civilian life. This would have been a full-time job for anyone but Winston. Once he got the demobilization working smoothly, he looked around for something else to do.

There was a revolution going on in Russia. Just a year before the end of the war, a party called the Bolsheviks, under their leaders, Lenin and Trotzky, had seized the Russian Government. They had deposed and murdered the Tsar and his family. The Bolsheviks were Communists.

Many of the Russian people did not like the new government. A civil war broke out.

In 1917, the Bolsheviks had made a separate peace with the Germans, while their allies were still fighting. Winston hated quitters, and he did not like Communism. He decided that it was England's duty to help the anti-Bolsheviks, and for that reason did not recall British troops already stationed in Russia.

But the Bolsheviks won, and Britain recognized the new government. What the English wanted was peace at any price. England was tired of fighting.

Most of the people in Europe felt the same way. They formed the League of Nations. All the mem-

Leon Trotsky outlived Nikolai Lenin by sixteen years, only to be murdered in Mexico.

A scene during the Russian Revolution.

bers of the League of Nations promised to arbitrate their disagreements and never go to war again.

The British people were glad to have their country join the League of Nations. They needed a chance to settle their troubles at home.

The Irish question, and the question of votes for women had to be dealt with. And English working people wanted laws to guarantee them higher wages, and better homes, and shorter hours, more safety in the mills, in the mines, in the factories. The Liberal Party could not push these measures through Parliament.

So a new party was taking shape — the Labor Party.

Winston had believed that the government should not enter into the everyday lives of people. He thought it was undemocratic. He never had been in sympathy with the Liberal Party's ideas about social reform. He left the Liberal Party.

He asked the Conservatives to take him back.

The Conservatives weren't really very anxious to have him. But he was so well known that they didn't dare refuse. They even gave him an unimportant post in their Cabinet.

Time for an election came around. The Liberals were snowed under and practically disappeared. The Conservatives made a good fight, but the Laborites won.

Winston stood as an Independent. He lost.

After two years, Winston was able to convince the Conservatives that they should take him back into the fold. When the party came back into power he was made Chancellor of the Exchequer.

He held this post for five years, but in 1929 the Labor Party took over, and Winston was out of the Cabinet again. And even though the Conservatives regained power later, Winston remained a plain M.P. for ten years.

During those years he lived in retirement at Chartwell, his country home.

Tame animals were all around him — not only horses and dogs and cats — but even chickens and ducks and goldfish. He was great friends with his four children. He joined in their hobbies. When he saw them painting, he tried his hand at that. He had such a good time that he bought himself a set of oil paints and a big floppy hat and a cream-colored smock. He carried his easel and his gear all over the countryside painting landscapes. He became quite a good painter indeed.

He started building a new wing on the house. He became so expert at bricklaying that he was invited to join the Bricklayers' Union.

Every afternoon he wrote. He turned out a book about his early life, and one about the Great War.

But most important of all, he began working on a biography of John Churchill, the First Duke of Marlborough.

Mr. and Mrs. Churchill also went traveling. They went to the places where the Duke of Marlborough had fought his battles. Many of these battlefields were in Germany.

What Winston saw there in 1932 stirred up his old feeling about Germany.

All over the world times were very bad. In the democracies, like England and France and the United States, people believed that the depression had come because of the Great War. They believed in peace. But in Italy and Germany, dictators were taking over. They told their people that bad times could be cured only by war.

After World War I, much territory had been taken away from Germany. She had lost the Ruhr and Alsace-Lorraine to France, and Schleswig-Holstein to Denmark. Her colonies had been given to France and England and even to Japan.

Hitler promised the Germans that he would get these possessions back for them. He promised

Winston became so proficient that he could qualify as a member of the Bricklayers' Union.

that he would annex Austria, Czechoslovakia, Poland, and any other place where Germans had gone to live. His party was called the National Socialist Party, NAZI for short.

Benito Mussolini (*Il Duce*) was the leader in Italy. Adolf Hitler (*Der Führer*) was the leader in Germany.

Hitler wrote a book called *Mein Kampf* (*My Battle*), in which he plainly told his plans. He told the Germans that they were supermen and should rule the world.

After the Great War, Germany had been made to sign a promise that she would not re-arm. But Winston had seen young people everywhere, both men and women, drilling and goose-stepping, just like an army. He had seen hundreds of German civilians learning to fly. They pretended they were only doing it for sport. He realized that all of them could be turned into a real army and a splendid air force at a moment's notice.

Winston had returned to England with his mind made up. He set up a whole private spy system for himself so he would know what was going on in Germany. He told everybody what he had found out about *Der Führer*. He made speeches. He begged everybody to read *Mein Kampf*. He tried to convince people that Hitler was getting ready for war.

But nobody listened to him.

The Parliament was busy trying to cure the depression. The English themselves were so anxious for peace that they couldn't believe anybody would think of anything else. Let the League of Nations take care of the warmongers, they said.

In 1932, Japan walked out of the League, marched into Manchuria, and took over.

In 1935, Mussolini's armies overran North Africa and annexed Ethiopia. Now Italy was out of the League.

In the same year, Hitler's army marched into

Il Duce addresses 25,000 people in Rome, 1932, on the 10th anniversary of the March on Rome.

Der Führer exhorts the audience at the Lustgarten meeting during the National Holiday of the German people, May 1, 1938.

the Rhineland, breaking the German Peace Treaty. A few months later that year, an alliance was formed between Germany, Italy, and Japan — the Rome-Berlin-Tokyo Axis.

Winston Churchill begged England to wake up. But still no one would listen to him.

The Russians proposed an alliance to the British and the French. Winston didn't like the Russians, but he knew they would make valuable allies in case of war against Germany. He urged that their proposition be accepted.

Negotiations dragged on and on.

Early in 1938, Hitler's armies occupied Austria, and annexed it. Then *Der Führer* demanded that Czechoslovakia give back to Germany a large slice of its country.

The British Prime Minister, Neville Chamberlain, flew to Munich to see Hitler. Appeasingly, Chamberlain agreed to let Hitler do what he wanted with helpless little Czechoslovakia if *Der Führer* would promise not to grab anything else.

Hitler promised.

Chamberlain came home, smiling and happy. There would be "peace in our time," he told the anxious English crowds waiting at the railway station.

But he was wrong.

Stalin, the Russian dictator, tired of waiting for England to make up her mind, suddenly announced a pact with Germany. Russia immediately started out to conquer Finland.

A week later, the Germans marched into Poland.

It took just three days for the great Nazi army to reduce Poland to ashes. The Germans called this a *Blitzkrieg* or lightning war. Then Russia and Germany carved up the beaten country. Germany took the west half, Russia the east.

This was too much for the French and the British. In September, 1939, they both declared war on Germany.

The infamous Munich Peace Parley, September 29, 1938. Left to right, Neville Chamberlain, Edouard Daladier, Adolf Hitler, Benito Mussolini and his son-in-law, Count Ciano, whom he later had executed.

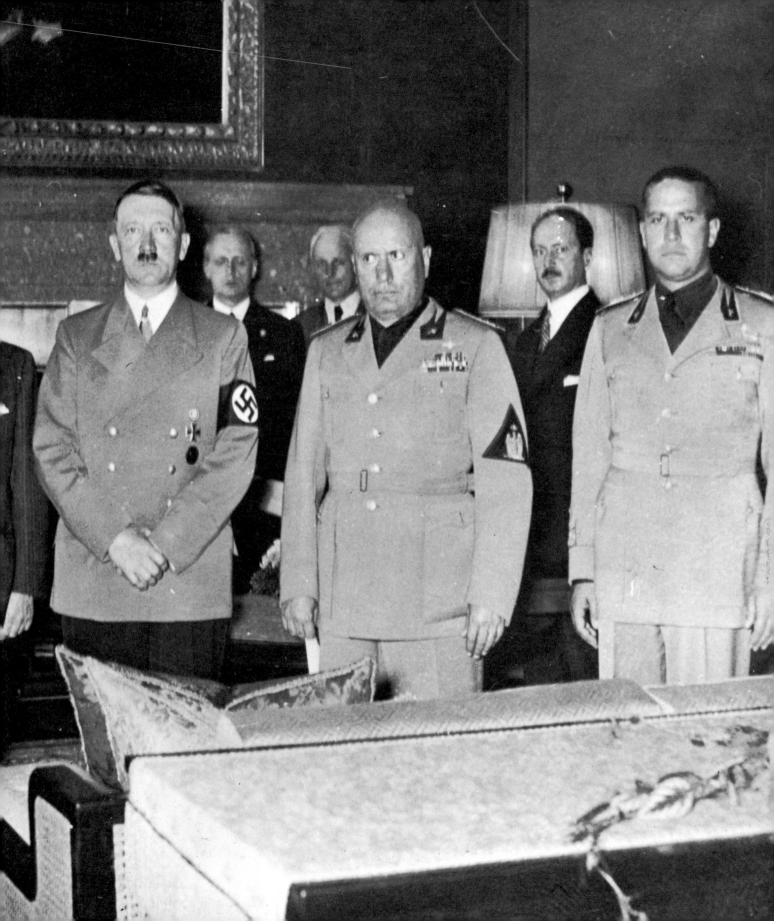

XIV. Prime Minister of England

"Winnie is back!"

This was the message signaled from battleship to battleship.

The moment England declared war, Prime Minister Chamberlain appointed Winston Churchill First Lord of the Admiralty.

It was as though the events of the last twenty-five years had never happened. As World War II began, Winston was back in the same position of authority that he had held when World War I started.

Winston at once deployed the battleships for combat, the small boats for U-boat chasing, other ships to range the seven seas in search of Nazi raiders, to transport the Army across the English Channel. It was like World War I.

But this time he had airplanes and airplane carriers too, ready for use.

Winston's navy was already in action before the rest of England was more than half awake.

The months dragged by. The English people slowly made ready for war. Remembering the Zeppelin raids and the dreadful poison gas of World War I, men, women, children, and even dogs and cats were given gas masks.

Men, and women, too, hurried to enlist. But their papers piled up on desks. Only a few troops actually reached France.

Hitler seemed in no hurry to start the fighting there. Between the wars, the French had built a long line of fortified trenches, the Maginot Line, on the border facing toward Germany. Later, the Germans had constructed similar trenches, the Siegfried Line, facing the French.

The opposing armies marched into these trenches, and settled down and waited.

For nine months, all was quiet on the Western Front. The British soldiers began singing about "Hanging Out the Washing on the Siegfried Line." Americans began talking about the "phony war."

Prime Minister Chamberlain made speeches about how this delay gave England time to mobilize. He forgot that Hitler was using the time the same way.

The Siegfried Line, the German border barrier, zigzags across the land.

The Dunkirk miracle—ships stand by to evacuate the troops wading out from shore.

"Hitler has missed the bus," proclaimed Mr. Chamberlain confidently.

Three days later, Hitler overran Denmark and seized Norway.

There was a great demonstration in Parliament. In the midst of the shouting, Mr. Chamberlain resigned.

That very night, May 10th, 1940, King George V sent for Winston Churchill and asked him to become Prime Minister of England.

History repeats itself as fires rage

Now at last Churchill was at the top. He was where his enormous talents — his obstinacy, his bravery, and his big ideas — could be most useful. Winston cut red tape everywhere. Quickly he enlarged the Army. He stepped up defense. Under his driving power, the whole nation buckled down to work.

He said, "I have nothing to offer you but blood, toil, tears, and sweat."

In May, 350,000 British soldiers were caught

through London during the Blitz.

Churchill walks the deck of HMS Prince of Wales *en route to the Atlantic Charter meeting with President Roosevelt, 1941.*

in a pocket at Dunkirk, on the Channel coast. Winston commandeered practically every British boat that would float to go after them. Dramatically, the Army escaped across the Channel.

Less than a month later, France fell to the Nazis. Now Britain stood alone against the Nazi might.

"We shall defend our island, whatever the cost may be," Churchill declared. "We shall fight on the beaches, we shall fight on the landing grounds, we shall fight in the fields and in the streets, we shall fight in the hills, we shall never surrender."

Churchill's fierce and moving speeches inspired millions of men and women to stand against the Nazi tyranny. His bulldog determination helped them in their fight for freedom.

He invented a signal. He would raise his right hand with his first two fingers spread, and make a "V for Victory." *Never give up!* This is what Winston's "V" held high above his head said to his countrymen.

In the months that followed, the Nazis blitzed the British Isles as they had blitzed Poland.

Bombs fell on the coast towns, on the inland towns, and London itself was half wiped out by fire. But the people of Britain stood fast.

Winston was everywhere — at blitzed-out homes, in air raid shelters, in fireswept streets — joking, sympathizing, and making his V sign.

When the German *Messerschmitts* roared overhead, the Royal Air Force, though fearfully outnumbered, went up and drove them back.

"Never," said Churchill, praising the Air Force, "in the field of human conflict was so much owed by so many to so few."

Day and night the Nazi planes came over spreading fire and death and destruction. They came from all directions, but they found the Royal Air Force was always ready for them.

The British had a secret weapon — radar. Radar

At alternate sessions held on the U.S
Roosevelt and Church

...gusta and HMS Prince of Wales ...on became good friends.

was an electronic device which plotted the course of every approaching plane.

When Churchill first heard of this new invention, he had jumped at the idea of adopting it for Britain's defense. Radar made it possible for the small British Air Force to win the Battle of Britain.

As Prime Minister, Churchill had a free hand. He took into his Cabinet the most able members of the Labor Party, so that the working people would back him up.

He arranged a meeting with Franklin Delano Roosevelt, President of the neutral United States. The two men met on the Atlantic Ocean on a battleship. Together they composed a new Bill of Rights for free men everywhere — the Four Freedoms — Freedom of Speech, Freedom of Worship, Freedom from Want, and Freedom from Fear.

At that meeting Churchill persuaded Roosevelt to lend him some American cruisers to guard English merchantmen carrying supplies. The Nazis were blockading England, and the English people were often short of food.

Without warning, Hitler invaded his former ally, Russia. And now the Soviet Union was in the war on Britain's side.

On December 7, 1941, Japan, a partner in the Axis, made a sneak attack on the United States at Pearl Harbor. The United States declared war on the Axis.

Churchill's V sign was becoming more than a symbol. It was becoming a promise.

He went to "Summit" meetings with Britain's allies, Roosevelt, Stalin, and Chiang Kai-shek of China. They met in North Africa, then in Canada, in Iran and in Russia. Stalin was a little suspicious of Churchill. The Russians could not forget that Winston had sent the British troops to fight against the Bolsheviks.

Churchill and Roosevelt became fast friends.

In many ways they were much alike. They both were "defiant in defeat," and both hated red tape.

Together, at the Summit meetings, the Allies planned grand strategy. They picked a day when the British and the Americans would invade the continent of Europe.

Churchill had other plans as well. He sparked an invasion of Italy by way of North Africa. And he suggested that the British and Americans together strike in the Balkans at what he called "the soft underbelly of Europe."

The North African-Italian campaign went forward.

A Summit meeting was held at Yalta on the Black Sea. The European invasion was almost ready to go. Churchill brought up his Balkan plan again.

Churchill, with his usual talent for hats, is shown at Yalta, Crimea, during the Three-Power Conference in February, 1945.

Stalin, Roosevelt, and Churchill, shown on the steps of the Russian Embassy in Teheran, Iran, plan to concentrate their combined military might on Germany.

But Stalin wanted the Balkans for himself. And Roosevelt was ill. He could no longer smooth things over between Churchill and Stalin. He gave in to Stalin, and the Balkan plan was scrapped.

June 6, 1944, was D-Day. The Allies landed in France.

Before a year had passed, Hitler fell. The Allied Forces took Germany. Roosevelt had died before V-E Day. The Americans had a new President, Harry S. Truman. Winston Churchill went to Potsdam to meet with Truman and Stalin and to plan the peace.

U.S. reinforcement troops wade from the landing craft to the Normandy shore.

XV. "Happily Ever Afterwards"

The war was over.

The British held an election, and the Labor Party won. In the British House of Commons, the Party with the biggest majority picks one of its members for Prime Minister.

Winston was a Conservative.

So Winston Churchill, who had steered his country through its greatest war, was no longer Prime Minister of Great Britain.

The whole world was stunned! Everywhere Churchill was the hero. How could the British do such a thing to such a man?

But Churchill was the most British of all the British. He wasn't happy about what had happened. But deep down inside he understood.

He knew that his countrymen still admired and trusted him as their great War Minister and believed in him in times of international trouble. But he also realized that many Englishmen had never been satisfied with the way his party handled matters at home.

Once in power, the Laborites set right to work to try to unscramble domestic problems. They tackled the food problem, and the housing, and re-employment of soldiers, and medical care. The Government took over the railroads, which had been hard hit by war, and the coal mines, and helped industries that were finding it hard to get back on a peace footing.

Churchill disapproved of almost all the Labor Party's measures. He was the Leader of the Opposition now. And he spoke his mind whenever he wanted to. Especially about how the government was acting in foreign affairs.

He advocated a Federation of Europe. He could not put it over. Everybody listened to his speeches and applauded them, but nobody took his advice.

He kept himself very busy writing a great history of World War II. He went on lecture tours. Now that the war was over, he could say whatever he pleased about Stalin and the Communists.

He went to America. He made a speech at Westminster College in the little town of Fulton, Missouri. He told his listeners how the Russians had promised to hold free elections in the Balkans, and in Poland where their victorious armies were. He said they had gone back on their promise, and that these countries were all Communist Russian dominated now. They were nothing more than Russian satellites.

A distinguished visitor to Fulton, Mo., Churchill rides through town with President Harry Truman in March of 1946.

Sir Winston Churchill kisses the hand of his Queen, 89] *Elizabeth II, at what is believed to be his last formal dinner at 10 Downing Street. Lady Churchill stands at the left.*

And Russia had dropped an iron curtain between the communist world and the free democracies of the West. Churchill's expression, "The Iron Curtain," became a part of the English language.

Things were better at home, but the dignity of Britain abroad was slipping. The British people were tired of the Laborites.

New elections were held. After two tries, the Conservatives got in.

In 1951, Winston Churchill, seventy-seven years old, was returned to Parliament as Prime Minister of Britain.

Making his world-famous "V" sign, he again became the First Statesman of the British people.

Now all the honors that he had earned by his stirring deeds were heaped upon him by the whole world. Elizabeth II, the young Queen of England, knighted him and gave him the Order of the Garter, the most ancient and desired decoration in English tradition. He was Sir Winston now, the most admired, the most beloved, the most talked about person in all the United Kingdom.

The whole world applauded.

Five years later, because he himself wished it, he resigned his office.

He kept his old seat in Parliament. He still wanted to be able to go back and speak his mind when he pleased.

In 1963, he was given honorary citizenship in the land of his mother's birth — the only person ever to have been so saluted by the Congress of the United States.

But most of his time he spent with his wife and his family, his writing, his painting, his gardening, and his animal friends.

And, as he himself said at the time he and Lady Churchill were married — they lived happily ever afterwards.

Winston carries an honorary Dr. of Laws degree conferred upon him by Westminster College, Fulton, Mo., only one of many received by the man who was "low boy" in his class.

"Palladian Bridge" was painted by Winston Churchill in 1925.

In Miami Beach, Florida, Winston combines two of his hobbies — painting, and puffing on his famous black cigar.

In Westminster Hall, London, Sir Winston receives the acclaim of both Houses of Parliament on his 80th birthday.

Partners for fifty-one years. Sir Winston and Lady Churchill in their London home, Hyde Park Gate, in November of 1959.